Looking After Me

Keeping Clean

Crabtree Publishing Company

www.crabtreebooks.com

Crabtree Publishing Company

www.crabtreebooks.com   1-800-387-7650

Copyright © **2009 CRABTREE PUBLISHING COMPANY.**

Published in Canada
Crabtree Publishing
616 Welland Ave.
St. Catharines, ON
L2M 5V6

Published in the United States
Crabtree Publishing
PMB16A
350 Fifth Ave., Suite 3308
New York, NY 10118

Senior editor
Jennifer Schofield

Proofreader
Crystal Sikkens

Designer
Sophie Pelham

Project coordinator
Robert Walker

Digital color
Carl Gordon

Production coordinator
Margaret Amy Salter

Editor
Molly Aloian

Prepress technician
Katherine Kantor

Copy editor
Adrianna Morganelli

First published in 2008 by Wayland
338 Euston Road
London NW1 3BH

Wayland Australia
Level 17/207 Kent Street
Sydney NSW 2000

Copyright © Wayland 2008

Wayland is a division of
Hachette Children's Books,
a Hachette Livre UK company.

Library and Archives Canada Cataloguing in Publication

Gogerly, Liz
    Keeping clean / Liz Gogerly ; illustrator, Mike Gordon.

(Looking after me)
Includes index.
ISBN 978-0-7787-4112-1 (bound).--ISBN 978-0-7787-4119-0 (pbk.)

    1. Hygiene--Juvenile fiction. I. Gordon, Mike II. Title. III. Series:
Gogerly, Liz. Looking after me.

PZ7.G562Ke 2008   j823'.92   C2008-903646-8

Library of Congress Cataloging-in-Publication Data

Gogerly, Liz.
    Keeping clean / written by Liz Gogerly ; illustrated by Mike Gordon.
      p. cm. -- (Looking after me)
    Includes index.
    ISBN-13: 978-0-7787-4119-0 (pbk. : alk. paper)
    ISBN-10: 0-7787-4119-2 (pbk. : alk. paper)
    ISBN-13: 978-0-7787-4112-1 (reinforced library binding : alk. paper)
    ISBN-10: 0-7787-4112-5 (reinforced library binding : alk. paper)
    1. Hygiene--Juvenile literature. I. Gordon, Mike, ill. II. Title.

RA780.G64 2009
613'.4--dc22

2008025346

Looking After Me

Keeping Clean

Written by Liz Gogerly
Illustrated by Mike Gordon

Karim and Kurt loved playing in dirt. Being mucky was marvelous. Getting grubby was great.

The dirty pair hated bath time.
Clean clothes felt horrible.

Kurt ran away
from hairbrushes.

Karim liked long
nails that could
scoop up dirt.

6

They often forgot
to clean their teeth.

But everything changed the day they visited the zoo. It began when they saw the bears.

"Why are they rubbing themselves like that?" asked Kurt. "To scratch off the dirt," explained his Dad.

9

The tigers were licking themselves clean with their bristly tongues.

The monkeys were
grooming each other.
They picked out
fleas, bits of dirt,
and leftover food.

Even the elephants were
washing themselves,
spraying water everywhere.

The giraffes' house was really smelly. But, the zookeeper went in with his hose and brush. The giraffes were soon much happier.

The zookeeper told the boys about wild animals. Crocodiles have their teeth cleaned by a little bird. It eats the scraps from between the crocodile's sharp teeth.

The boys enjoyed
their trip to the zoo.
It made them think
about keeping clean.

If animals could wash
themselves, so could they.

Kurt and Karim cleaned up their acts.
Now they wash, soap, and dry their hands
after they've been to the bathroom.

Before and after eating,
they clean their hands.

If there isn't any water, they use a special gel instead.

They rub and rub until all the gel is gone.

It's important to get
rid of the germs.

Germs are like little bugs
that live on your skin.

They can make
you very sick.

These days,
Kurt takes
more showers.

Karim's discovered
that baths can be
a lot of fun.

Afterward, it's important to dry from head to toe. If they don't, their skin might itch.

Then they put on nice, clean pajamas.
They feel soft and smell fresh.

These days,
Kurt brushes
his teeth
every morning
and night.

Karim lets his Dad
cut his nails. Short
nails are cleaner
and have
less germs.

They put on
clean underwear
and clothes
every morning.

Once a week, they both
get out the shampoo.
It makes their hair shine.

27

Then it's off to have fun and get covered in mud, muck, grass stains, and scrapes.

NOTES FOR PARENTS AND TEACHERS

SUGGESTIONS FOR READING
LOOKING AFTER ME: KEEPING CLEAN
WITH CHILDREN

Keeping Clean is the story of two boys called Kurt and Karim. Like many young children, they try to avoid washing, having their hair and teeth brushed, and having their nails trimmed. The story begins with a few amusing scenes where the boys' parents attempt to groom their wayward sons. After reading this early section, you could discuss with the children their own personal hygiene habits. This could be a lively debate as children love to talk about being dirty and grubby.

Kurt and Karim change their attitude toward keeping clean when they visit the zoo. The children may have their own experiences of watching animals groom themselves. They could talk about how their pets keep clean. Possibly, they've seen birds taking baths in the garden. Talking about animals is always a good way of getting children to open up on a subject. This would be a useful way of starting a discussion about why the children think it is important to keep clean.

It is important for children to learn when to wash their hands and how to do this properly. The book has different examples of Kurt and Karim washing their hands. The children may have other examples of when to wash their hands, too. This is a good time to talk to the children about germs and infections and how keeping themselves, and especially their hands, clean helps to prevent illnesses.

By the end of the book, Kurt and Karim enjoy bathing and grooming and know the reasons why they should keep clean. However, it's important that children are allowed to explore the world around them. Getting dirty is part of that process and there is rarely any harm in getting covered in dirt, if they have a good wash afterward!

LOOKING AFTER ME AND CURRICULUM EXPECTATIONS

The Looking After Me series is designed to teach young readers the importance of personal hygiene, proper nutrition, exercise, and personal safety. This series supports key K-4 health education standards in Canada and the United States, including those outlined by the American Association for Health Education. According to these standards, students will

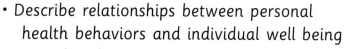

- Describe relationships between personal health behaviors and individual well being
  - Explain how childhood injuries and illnesses can be prevented or treated
    - Identify responsible health behaviors
    - Identify personal health needs
    - Demonstrate strategies to improve or maintain personal health
  - Demonstrate ways to avoid and reduce threatening situations

31

BOOKS TO READ

Health Choices: Keeping Clean
Cath Senker (Wayland, 2004)
Me and My Body: Why Wash?
Claire Llewellyn (Wayland, 2008)
Dirty Bertie David Roberts
(Little Tiger Press, 2003)

ACTIVITY

Using the examples of the bears, tiger, monkeys, and crocodiles in this book, ask children to look for pictures of different animals cleaning themselves. They could find examples of both domestic animals, such as cats that lick themselves, or wild animals, such as buffaloes that have a secretary bird to pick bugs from their hides.

INDEX

Printed in China